W9-BNQ-245

INDIAN AMERICANS

Robin Doak

AMERICAN IMMIGRANTS

Rourke
Publishing LLC
Vero Beach, Florida 32964

www.rourkepublishing.com

PHOTO CREDITS: Courtesy of the Bancroft Library, University of California: p. 16; Ghubert Banta, Curtis Irish, Stephen Williamson: pp. 13, 18; Bettman/Corbis: p. 10; Rob Bowden/EASI Images/CFW Images: p. 7; Bojan Brecelj/Corbis: p. 27; Discovery Picture Library: p. 28; Chris Fairclough/CFW Images: p. 5; Keystone Features/Getty Images: p. 8; Andrew Lichtenstein/Corbis: p. 43; David McNew/Getty Images: p. 40; Ethan Miller/Getty Images: p. 34; Gail Mooney/Corbis: p. 22; Kelly Mooney Photography/ Corbis: p. 30; NASA: pp. 36, 38; Suman Rawal: pp. 29, 33; A. J. Sisco/Corbis: p. 37; Vancouver Public Library: p. 12; David H. Wells/Aurora/Getty Images: p. 21; David H. Wells/Corbis: pp. 23, 41.

Cover picture shows two Indian dancers at the Festival of India in Middlesex County, New Jersey [Kelly Mooney Photography/Corbis].

Produced for Rourke Publishing by Discovery Books
Editor: Gill Humphrey
Designer: Ian Winton
Photo researcher: Rachel Tisdale

Library of Congress Cataloging-in-Publication Data

Doak, Robin S. (Robin Santos), 1963-
Indian Americans / Robin Doak.
p. cm. -- (American immigrants)
Includes bibliographical references.
Audience: Grades 4-6.
ISBN 978-1-60044-612-2
1. East Indian Americans--History--Juvenile literature. 2. East Indian Americans--Social conditions--Juvenile literature. 3. Immigrants--United States--History--Juvenile literature. 4. Immigrants--United States--Social conditions--Juvenile literature. 5. United States--Emigration and immigration--Juvenile literature. 6. India--Emigration and immigration--Juvenile literature. I. Title.
E184.E2D63 2008
973.0491'4--dc22

2007020170

Printed in the USA

TABLE OF CONTENTS

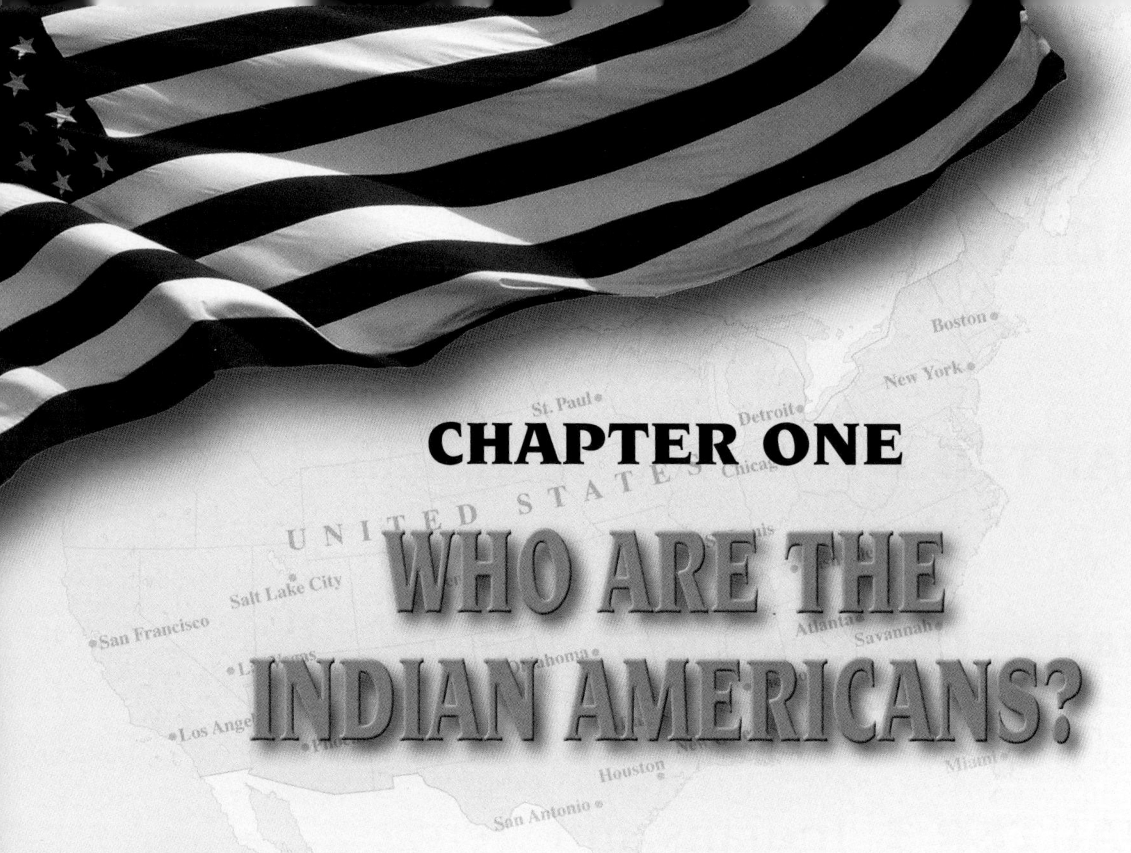

CHAPTER ONE

WHO ARE THE INDIAN AMERICANS?

Indian Americans are people who came from India to live in the United States. Their children, born in the United States, are Indian Americans too. India is a large country in South Asia. It has a very large **population**. Only China has more people.

The Geography and History of India

Most of India is a peninsula. A peninsula is a piece of land that is almost entirely surrounded by water. Much of India is bordered by

FUN FACTS ABOUT INDIA

- Animals found in India include tigers, elephants, leopards, peacocks, cobras, and monkeys.
- The first game of chess may have been played in India more than 1,000 years ago.
- Seven out of every ten Indians live in the nation's crowded cities.
- India is about one-third the size of the United States.

A crowded street in Delhi, the capital city of India.

the Indian Ocean. In the northern part of the country, the Himalaya Mountains separate the country from Nepal and China. The climate in this part of the nation is **temperate**, or mild. In the south, the land is flatter and good for farming. The climate here is **tropical**, or hot and damp.

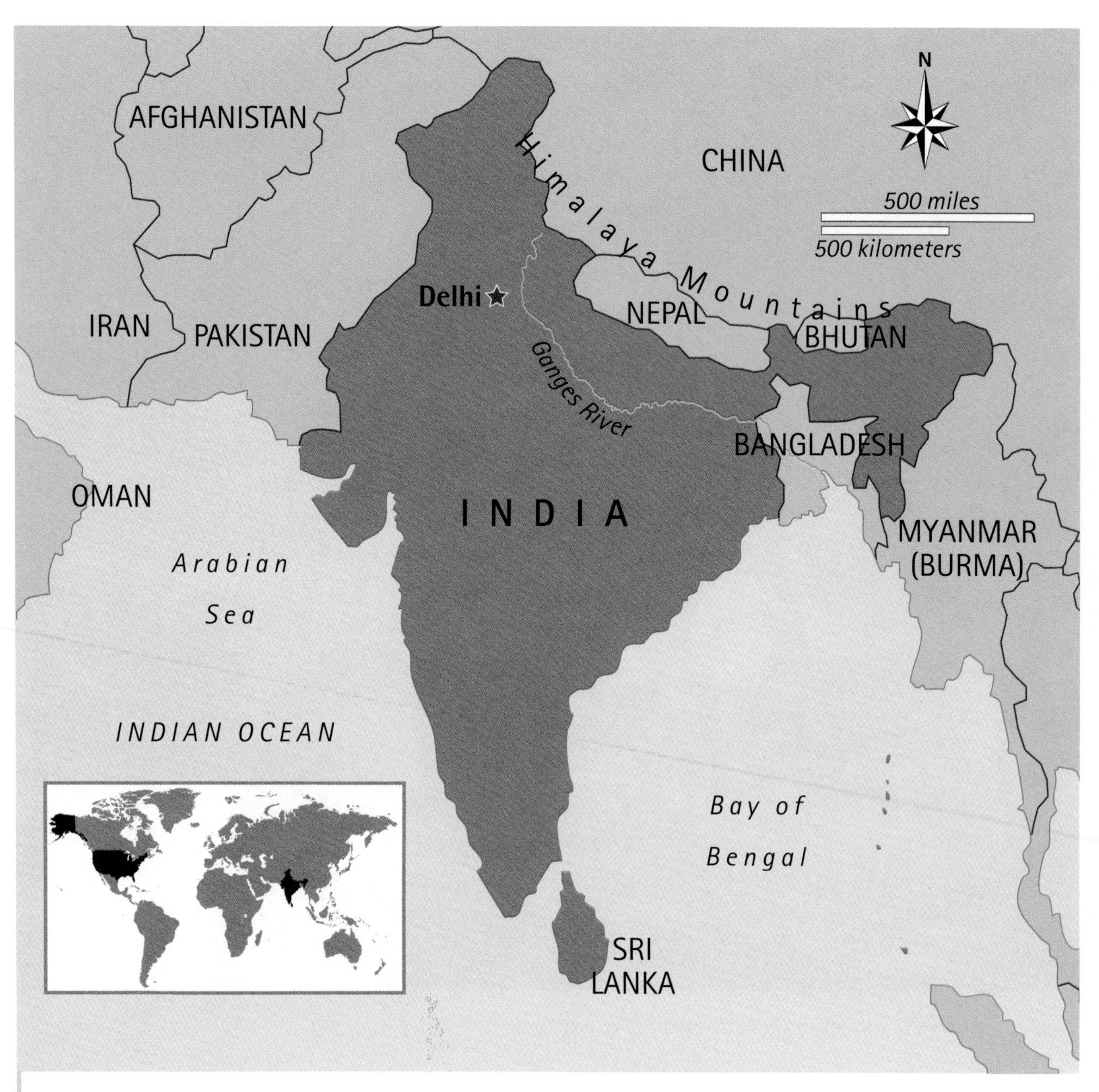

India is a large country in South Asia. It is the biggest ***democracy*** *in the world.*

(Opposite) Hindus visit a temple to worship their gods. They may bring the gods gifts of food and clothing. Most Hindus also have a shrine in their homes.

India is divided into 28 states and 7 territories. Each region has its own language and **culture**. Hindi is the national language of India. English is also commonly used by people there.

Religion is very important to most Indians. Eight out of ten people in the country are Hindu. Hindus believe in many different forms of god. Other religious groups in India include **Muslims**, Christians, and **Sikhs**.

People have lived in India for more than 9,000 years. Over time, the region was invaded by people from Central Asia and the Middle East. These conquerors brought their languages and **customs** with them to India. In 1858, Great Britain took control of the land that is now India, Pakistan, Bangladesh, and Sri Lanka. It became part of the **British Empire**. The British forced Indians to learn the English language and to adopt British customs.

Independence and Development

India won its freedom from Great Britain in 1947. At that time, the region was divided into the mostly Hindu Republic of India and a smaller Muslim state called Pakistan. In 1971, a **civil war** in Pakistan resulted in the creation of a new nation called Bangladesh.

India is a developing country. This means that the nation is working to overcome serious problems, like poverty, poor health care, and high numbers of people who cannot find jobs. India is one of the poorest nations in the world.

(Opposite) In 1947, India and Pakistan became two separate nations. This photograph shows Muslims about to board a special train that will take them to a new life in Pakistan.

MOHANDAS GANDHI

India's struggle for independence from British rule was led by Mohandas Gandhi. Gandhi believed that the best way to win freedom for India was to disobey unfair laws, but in a peaceful manner. He led marches, protests, and demonstrations to pressure the British government into freeing his country. Gandhi was also given the name "Mahatma," which means "Great Spirit" in Sanscrit. Sanscrit is the ancient language of India. In 1948, Gandhi was **assassinated** by a Hindu fanatic.

Mohandas Gandhi (center) leads his followers on a 200-mile (320-km) march for Indian rights. Gandhi is considered the father of modern India.

CHAPTER TWO

COMING TO THE UNITED STATES

The first Indians came to the United States around 1820. Most of these early **immigrants** were adventurers, merchants, or monks from northern India. In 1900, larger numbers of Indian immigrants began arriving here. Most of these new arrivals were Sikh men from the Punjab, a farming region in northern India.

Jobs for Immigrants

The early Indian immigrants arrived in Canada, then came to the

AN EARLY ARRIVAL

In 1790, a colonial minister reported seeing an Indian in Salem, Massachusetts. The Indian came to the United States as the servant of a ship's captain. The minister wrote, "Had the pleasure of seeing for the first time a native of the Indies....He is of dark complexion [skin], long straight black hair, soft countenance [features of the face], tall and well proportioned."

Many early immigrants traveled from India to Canada. Here, Sikh immigrants are shown at the port of Vancouver in southwestern Canada.

United States in search of jobs. Many worked in lumber mills in Washington and Oregon. Others worked on the Western Pacific Railroad in California. Later, Indians found jobs in Southern California as farm workers.

(Opposite) These Sikh men settled in Oregon in the early 1900s. They worked in the area's lumber mills.

During the early 1900s, many Indian immigrants came to the United States through the Angel Island Immigration Station in San Francisco.

These immigrants were mostly poor and uneducated. Few could speak English. They lived together in work camps, sleeping in shacks with dirt floors or in tents. However, the Indian Americans worked together to survive. They shared their wages, food, and supplies. Some of their money was sent back to India, to help those at home. Any extra money was used to buy land.

WHO ARE THE SIKHS?

Sikhs are members of a religious group that was founded in northern India in the late 1400s. The word *Sikh* means "learner" or "disciple" in an Indian language. Sikhs follow the teachings of a guru, or spiritual leader. Sikh men living outside India are often noticed because they wear **turbans**.

Arriving in a New Land

After 1910, Indians traveled by steamship to California. Their first stop was the Angel Island Immigration Station in San Francisco Bay. Here, their travel documents were checked. The immigrants were examined by doctors to make sure they were healthy. It was normal for newly-arrived immigrants to spend two or three weeks at Angel Island.

At this time, a U.S. law stated that only "free white men" could become U.S. citizens. Because of their dark skin, Indians were considered non-white and so were not allowed to become American citizens. They were also prevented from bringing their relatives or wives to the United States.

In the early 1900s, a small group of Indians came to the United States because they were unhappy with British rule in India. These early immigrants wanted India to be its own independent nation. They worked for India's freedom from their new home in the United States.

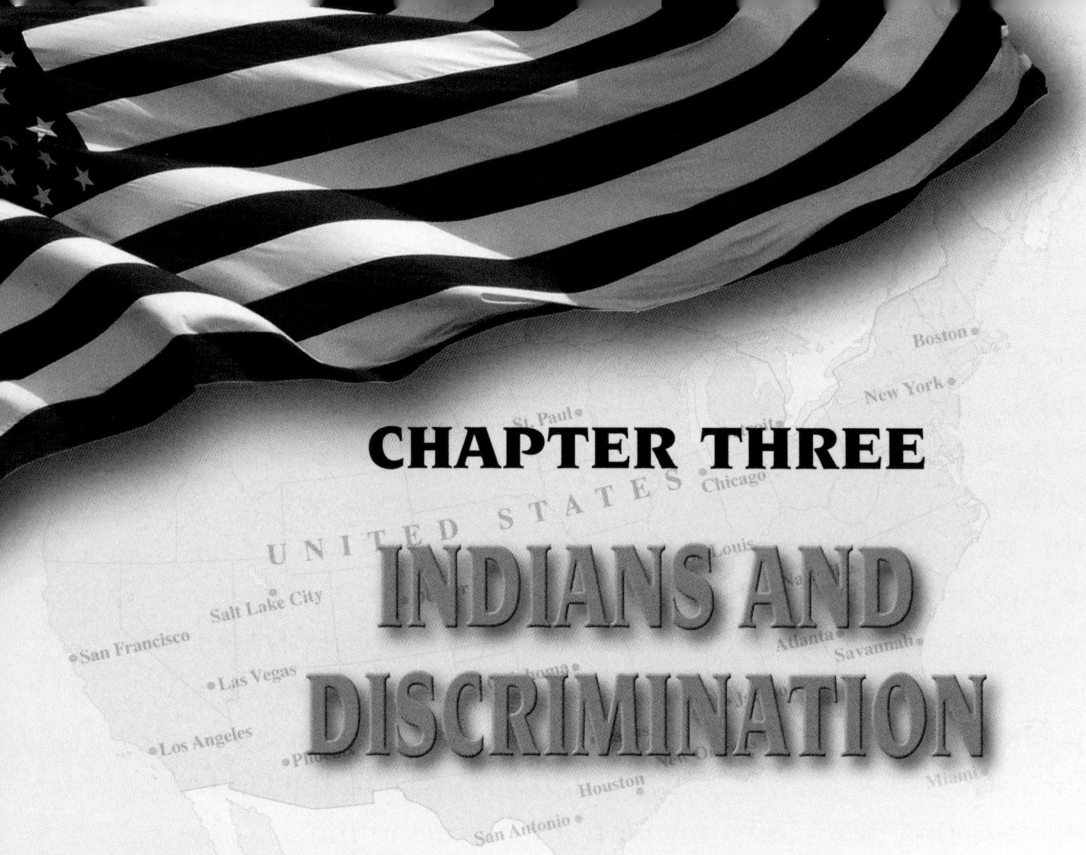

CHAPTER THREE

INDIANS AND DISCRIMINATION

Americans on the West Coast resented the new arrivals from India. White workers did not want Indians taking their jobs. The dark skin, full beards, and turbans of the Sikh immigrants also set them apart from other Americans.

A Difficult Time

In 1905, white workers in San Francisco formed a group to stop people **emigrating** from India, China, and other places in Asia. Two years later, nearly 1,000 Indians in Bellingham,

A cartoon from a 1910 San Francisco newspaper shows how some Americans viewed Indian immigrants. Not everyone agreed with that image. Dr. S. H. Lawson, a ship's surgeon who met many Indians said, "The Sikhs impressed me as a clean, manly, honest race."

THE GHADAR PARTY

In 1913, Sikhs in San Francisco, California, founded a political party called Ghadar, or "Mutiny." Ghadar's chief goal was to free India from British rule. In 1914, some members of the group went back to India in order to start a **revolution** against the British. Their plans failed, and many were put in jail or hanged.

Washington, were attacked and beaten by a mob of more than 400 white men.

Indians were also **discriminated** against in other ways. They were not permitted to eat at some restaurants or stay in certain hotels. In some places, laws prevented Indians from buying land.

The U.S. government also passed laws that discriminated against people from India and other Asian nations. In 1917, the government passed a law that limited the number of Asian people who could come to the United States. Then, in 1923, the Supreme

A poster showing the faces of some of the members of the Ghadar Party.

An early Sikh immigrant poses for a photo in his working clothes.

Court took away the citizenship of Asian Americans in the United States. The following year, a federal law ended all immigration from India and other Asian nations.

Immigration Laws and Citizenship

In 1946, immigration laws were changed to allow small numbers of people from India to emigrate to the United States. The same year, Indians were allowed to apply for U.S. citizenship. As a result, people from India once again began coming to the United States. Many settled on the West Coast. Others settled in places like New York, Chicago, and Detroit.

FIGHTING FOR FAIRNESS

Bhagat Singh Thind came to the United States from India in 1913. He worked in an Oregon lumber mill, attended a California university, and served in the U.S. Army during World War I. In 1920, he was granted U.S. citizenship in Oregon. Three years later, however, the U.S. Supreme Court ruled that Thind could not be a citizen because he was not white. Thind remained in the United States and was eventually awarded his citizenship in 1936.

Bhagat Singh Thind's brave military service during World War I was not enough to gain him U.S. citizenship.

CHAPTER FOUR

THE NEWEST U.S. CITIZENS

In 1965, Indians began coming to the United States in larger numbers than ever before. That year, a new U.S. law allowed more people to emigrate to the United States from India. By 1970, about 30,000 people had arrived here from India.

INDIANS FROM UGANDA

Not all Indian Americans who arrived after 1965 came directly from India. In 1972, more than 2,000 people of Indian **descent** were thrown out of the African nation of Uganda by the **dictator** Idi Amin. Some of these **refugees** came to the United States.

*(Opposite) In cities with large Indian populations, Indian Americans can shop in clothing stores for **saris** and other traditional Indian clothing.*

YOUR AGENT FOR
DOMESTIC
&
INTERNATIONAL
FOR RENT
INQUIRE WITHIN
BLANKETS PLUS
JACK 917-301-5738
FOR RENT
INQUIRE WITHIN
BLANKETS PLUS
JACK - 917-301-5738
Salwar-Kameez
Sherwanis
Jodhpuris

Indian restaurants have become popular with Americans of all backgrounds. In the Little India section of East Greenwich Village, New York, diners have many restaurants to choose from.

Educated Immigrants

Many of the people who came after 1965 were well-educated **professionals**. They were trained in India to be engineers, physicians, scientists, professors, teachers, and business people. They moved to

(Opposite) Celebrating religious holidays like Diwali is one way that Indian Americans stay connected with their roots. Diwali is the Hindu festival of lights.

the United States to earn more money than they could in India.

The new immigrants invited friends and family members to join them in the United States. These later arrivals had less schooling, but they were willing to work hard. Many started small businesses in the United States.

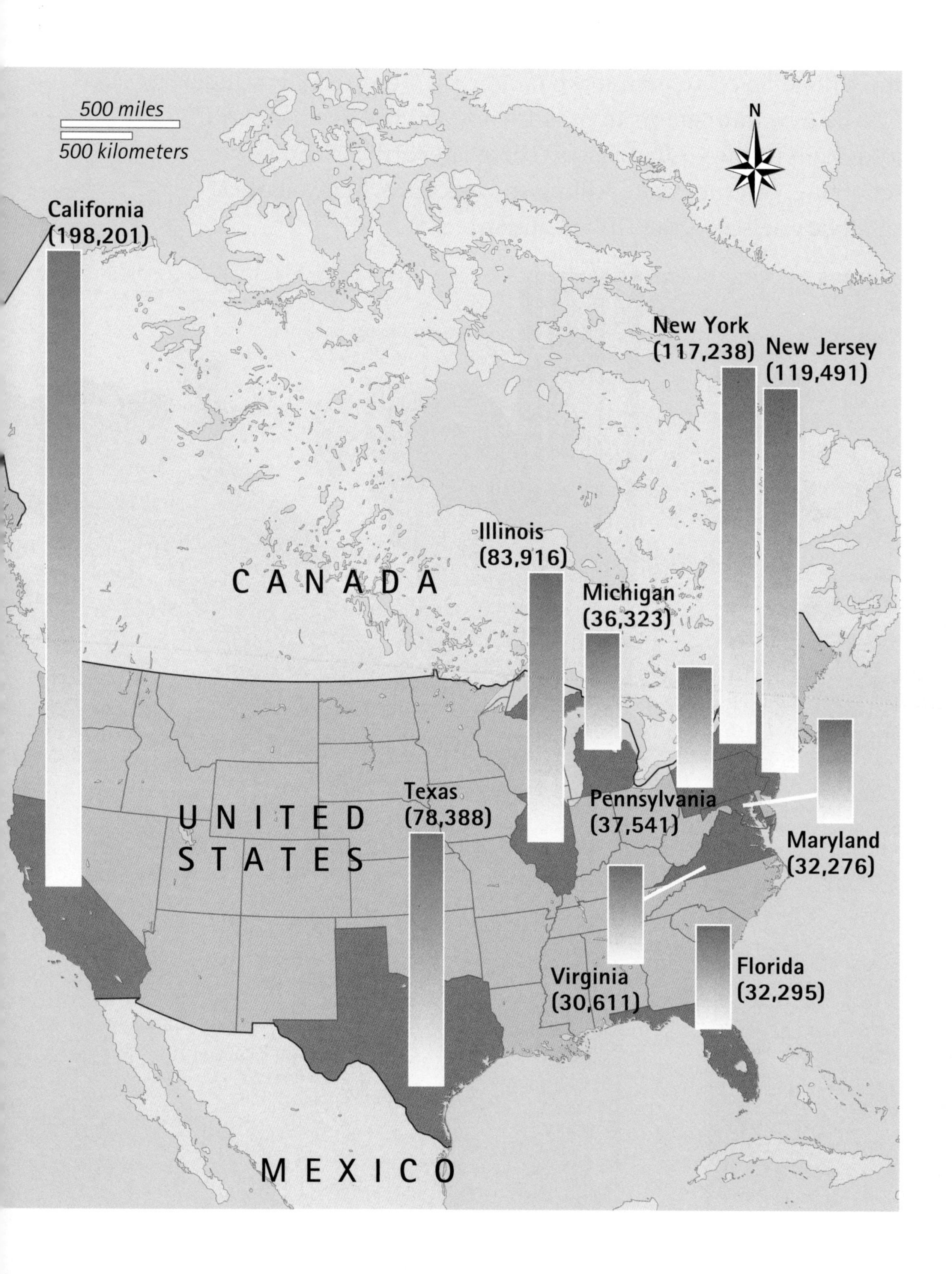
500 miles
500 kilometers
N
California
(198,201)
New York
(117,238)
New Jersey
(119,491)
Illinois
(83,916)
CANADA
Michigan
(36,323)
Texas
(78,388)
UNITED
STATES
Pennsylvania
(37,541)
Maryland
(32,276)
Virginia
(30,611)
Florida
(32,295)
MEXICO

The newest immigrants from India settled in the nation's major cities. Here, they could more easily find housing and jobs. Many Indians settled in New York and Chicago setting up groceries, restaurants, and other businesses. Indian neighborhoods became known as "Little Indias."

Family Life and Adapting to American Ways

Family life was important to the new immigrants. Many new arrivals moved in with family members who were already settled in the United States. Parents stayed with their adult children. They helped out by cooking, cleaning, or caring for their grandchildren.

Religion was also important. Hindus and Sikhs worshipped in temples. The temples were also used for community meetings, lectures, dances, and classes.

Indian immigrants had to adjust to life in a new land. Women took on new roles in the United States. Instead of staying home and caring for the family, many now found jobs. Some chose to dress like other American women instead of wearing the traditional sari. Men too began adopting some American customs.

(Opposite) States with the largest numbers of foreign-born Indians.

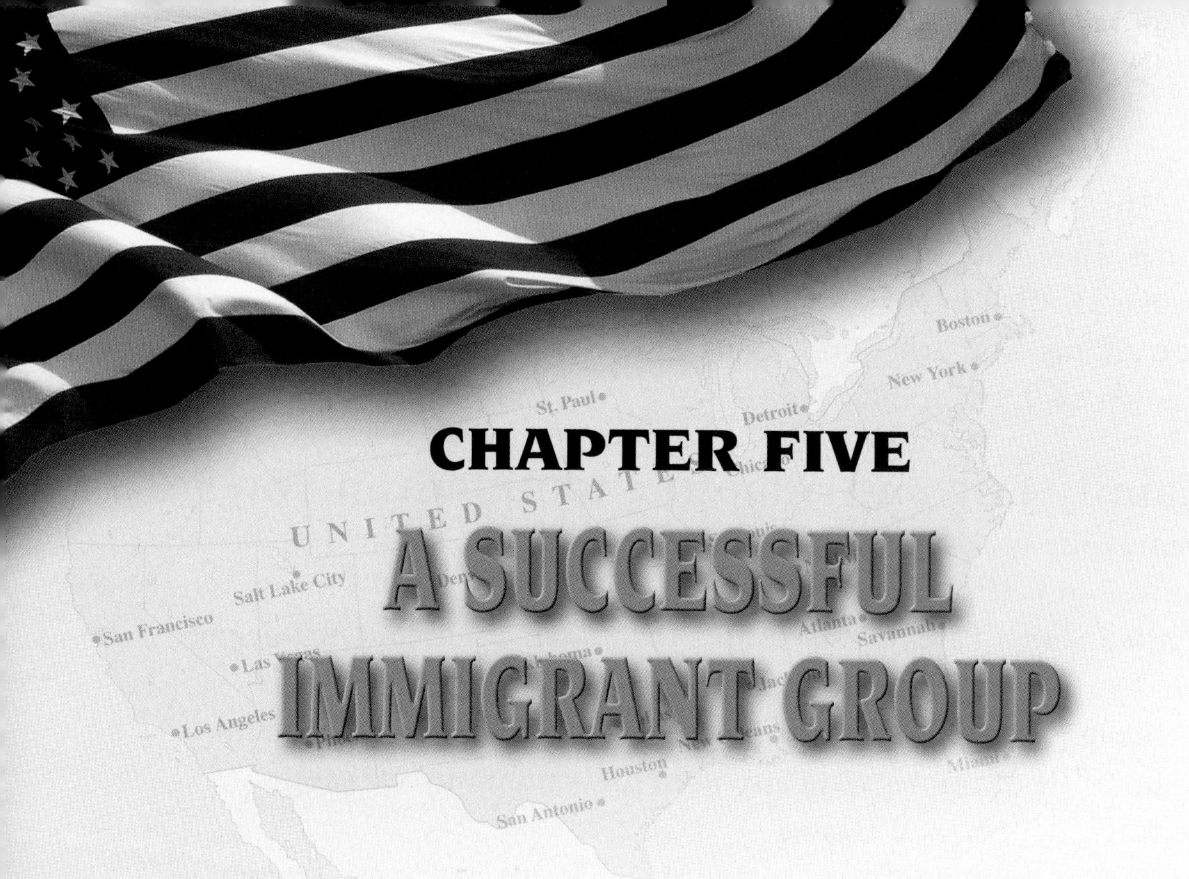

CHAPTER FIVE

A SUCCESSFUL IMMIGRANT GROUP

Indian Americans are one of the most successful immigrant groups in the United States. Many Indian immigrants can already speak English when they arrive in the U.S. They find it easier to fit in than some other immigrants. Indian Americans perform all types of jobs in the United States. They are doctors, scientists, and professors. They are also small business owners, waiters, and taxi drivers.

Indian Americans have been very successful in the field of computers and technology. They have also had great success as hotel owners. Today, four out of every ten hotels in the United States are owned by Indian Americans.

HELPING OTHERS

Indian Americans are generous to Indians in need. In 2001, a terrible earthquake in Gujarat, India, killed about 30,000 people. Thousands more were injured or left homeless. In California, Indian Americans raised more than $2 million to help the earthquake victims.

In New York City, some Sikh men drive taxis for a living.

Indian Americans hold all types of jobs. This Sikh man is an optician, someone who sells eyeglasses or contact lenses.

Keeping their Culture Alive

Indian Americans work hard to keep their language and culture alive. At home, Indian parents may speak their native tongue, serve traditional foods, and try to follow Indian customs. But many children of immigrants think of themselves as Americans first and Indians second. They are less willing to follow all of the customs of their parents.

ON MARRYING

Megha and her family came to the United States when she was just nine years old. Megha says she feels more American than Indian. But she knew that she would one day marry an Indian man. She said, "I wanted to be with someone who understands my culture, who knows what it is like to grow up Indian American."

*A photograph of Megha on her wedding day. Hindu weddings include both religious **rituals** and celebration. The ceremony is performed by a holy man and family members take part in the ceremony.*

In cities with large Indian-American communities, immigrants and their children attend programs that celebrate Indian language, music, and dance. They can watch a movie from India at a local theater or hall. There are television and radio shows, and newspapers and magazines that cater to Indian Americans. Indian festivals such as Durga-puja in Central Park, or the India Day Parade in New York City, are a time of celebration enjoyed by Indians and non-Indians alike.

Helping People in India

Many Indian Americans want to help those back in India. In 2001, Indians in the United States sent more than $9 million to households in India. Most of the money is sent directly to family members. They use this money to open new businesses, buy land, or repair their farms and homes.

FUTURE GENERATIONS

Hina emigrated to the U.S and settled in Detroit, Michigan, when she was nineteen. Now pregnant with her first child, Hina realizes that passing on Indian customs will be difficult. "I'm sure my kids will be less interested in keeping the traditions than I was," she says. "I'll do the best I can to make sure they understand Indian ways."

(Opposite) At celebrations like the Festival of India in New Jersey, Americans can enjoy Indian arts and culture.

CHAPTER SIX

ENRICHING OUR CULTURE

Americans can enjoy samples of Indian culture right here in the United States. Every day, for example, thousands of Americans take part in yoga classes. Yoga is a type of exercise that was developed by Hindus in India.

Fashion and Food

Indian fashions are also popular with some Americans. Pop stars like Madonna and Gwen Stefani have worn the bindi and mehndi. The

HENNA

Henna is a leaf that has been used in India for thousands of years. The leaf is crushed to make a brown paste. The paste is then painted on the skin with a brush or other tool. Today, Indian-American women often receive henna tattoos on special occasions.

A bride shows the mehndi patterns that were drawn on her hands for her wedding ceremony.

Film director M. Night Shyamalan accepts an award for Director of the Year in 2006.

bindi is the dot that some Indian women wear on their forehead. It can be a symbol of celebration. Mehndi are temporary henna tattoos. These tattoos are often painted on the feet and hands.

Thousands of Americans enjoy delicious Indian foods. At Indian restaurants, diners can order special flatbreads called roti and naan. They can dip them in a spicy **daal** or eat **curry** served with rice. Indian grocery stores sell all the ingredients people need to create their own Indian meals.

Books and Movies

Indian-American men and women have made important contributions to culture in the United States. There are many well-known writers, including children's author Dhan Gopal Mukerji (1890-1936). Mukerji won the 1928 Newberry Award for the book *Gay-Neck, the Story of a Pigeon.*

Indian Americans have also been successful in Hollywood. M. Night (Manoj Nelliyattu) Shyamalan (1970-) is a successful screenwriter and director. He created the movies *The Sixth Sense* and *Lady in the Water.*

OM DUTTA SHARMA

Om Dutta Sharma (1933-) was a successful lawyer when he left India in 1974. In the United States, however, Sharma could not practice law. So he began driving a cab. Sharma worked hard and saved money to help people in India. He used his savings to open a school for girls in India. He named the school for his mother, who never learned to read. Every month, Sharma sends money to pay the teachers who work at the school.

Astronaut Kalpana Chawla (center) was a crewmember on the 28th mission of the space shuttle Columbia *in 2003. Sadly, Chawla and her crewmates died when* Columbia *broke apart as it re-entered the Earth's atmosphere.*

Business, Science, and Politics

Indian Americans have made their marks in the business and science worlds. One of the most successful Indian businessmen is Sabeer Bhatia (1969-). Bhatia and a partner created Hotmail, the world's first public email program. National Aeronautics and Space Administration (NASA) astronaut Kalpana Chawla (1961-2003) was the first Indian American to fly a space shuttle mission.

Some Indian Americans have become involved in politics. The first Indian American elected to the U.S. Congress was Dalip Singh Saund (1899-1973) in 1956. Saund, a Punjabi Sikh, served three terms as a representative from California.

In 2007, Louisiana Republican Piyush "Bobby" Jindal was the only Indian American serving in the U.S. Congress.

A PRIZE-WINNING SCIENTIST

In 1983, Indian-born physicist Subrahmanyan Chandrasekhar (1910-1995) was awarded the **Nobel Prize** in Physics. He was given the prize for his research on stars. NASA's Chandra X-ray Observatory, launched into space in 1999, is named for him.

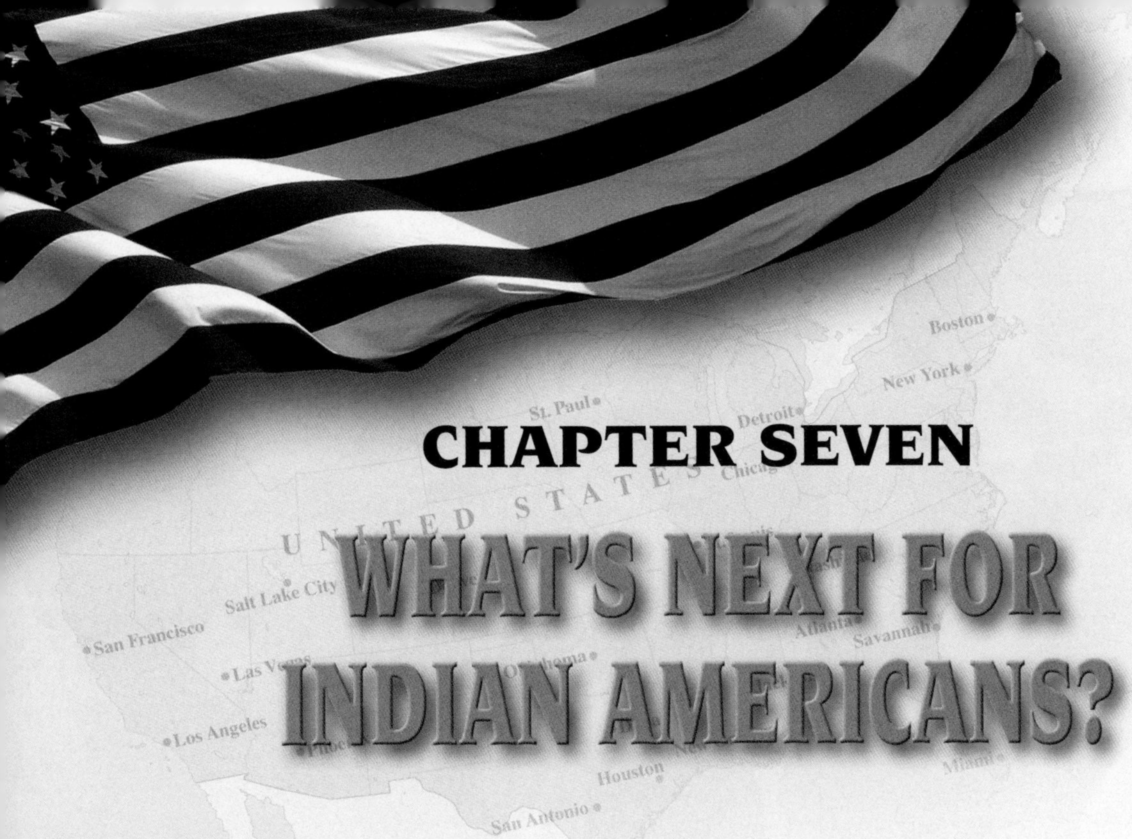

CHAPTER SEVEN

WHAT'S NEXT FOR INDIAN AMERICANS?

Indians continue to leave their homeland to escape poverty and other problems there. Between 2001 and 2004, nearly 262,000 people came to the United States from India. Many of the most recent arrivals from India are highly educated. Nearly seven out of every ten Indian immigrants has finished college.

The United States is now home to a large population of Indian Americans. In 2000, 1.6 million people of Indian descent lived here. They are setting up businesses, building temples, and sharing their culture with other Americans.

September 11, 2001, and Racial Prejudice

Prejudice against Indian Americans persists. After the September 11, 2001 **terrorist** attacks in New York, Washington, D.C., and Pennsylvania, some Americans became suspicious of anyone they

(Opposite) The Chandra X-ray Observatory was named for scientist Subrahmanyan Chandrasekhar.

Sikhs in Santa Ana, California attend a memorial service for victims of terrorist attacks.

(Opposite) Indian-American children learn about the United States and India at a school in Lowell, Massachusetts.

believed might be Muslim. Sikh men who wore turbans became the targets of hatred and violent attacks in some places.

Since 2001, Indian Americans have become more active in politics and in their communities. They want to show that they are important members of American society. In 2003, college students Anup Patel and Rina Patel founded an organization called Cents of Relief. The group raises money for **AIDS** victims in India.

KEEPING IN TOUCH WITH INDIA

Fifteen-year-old Sima was born in the United States, but her parents have taken her to India three times. Sima loves India, even though it is very different from the United States. Her grandmother's village has no paved roads and the electricity goes out every day for an hour or two. But when she is back in Maine, she misses her relatives. She also misses the delicious food. "It just tastes better there," Sima says.

A Positive Contribution

Indian Americans have played an important role in U.S. history. They have faced hostility and prejudice from Americans. But they did not give up. Recent Indian immigrants have been more warmly welcomed. These hard-working people have shown that they are good citizens and have contributions to make to our nation. They value the same things that other Americans value: family, education, and success. Today, Indian Americans are finding ways to show their pride in being both American and Indian.

HOMESICK FOR THE UNITED STATES

Indian Americans try to stay connected to India by making visits there. Megha has returned to her birth country once since coming to the United States. She said, "It was good to see relatives and friends." But she also felt homesick for the United States. "Things are so different over there," Megha said. "To the people in India, I'm an American. I really looked forward to coming home."

Two generations of Indian Americans watch the India Day Parade in New York City.

GLOSSARY

AIDS — Acquired Immune Deficiency Syndrome (uh KWIRED i MYOON di FISH uhnt see SIN drohm) — a serious condition that can lead to infections, cancer, and weakening of the nervous system

assassinated (uh SASS uh nay tid) — murdered, usually for political reasons

British Empire (BRIT ish EM pire) — a large number of countries controlled by Britain until the middle of the twentieth century

civil war (siv il wor) — a war between two factions within the same nation

culture (KUHL chur) — ideas, customs, and traditions

curry (KUH ree) — a dish made with spices

custom (KUHSS tuhm) — a way of behaving

daal (DAWL) — a dish made with grains, chickpeas, lentils, and beans

democracy (di MOK ruh see) — a form of government where the people elect their leaders

descent (di SENT) — coming from a family or ethnic group

dictator (DIK tay tur) — a ruler with complete power over his or her people

discrimination (diss krim i NAY shuhn) — showing unfair treatment toward a minority group

emigrate (EM uh grate) — to leave one's country and go to live in another; in the new country that person is an immigrant

immigrant (IM uh gruhnt) — person who has moved to another country to start a new life

Muslim (MUHZ luhm) — someone who follows the religion of Islam

Nobel Prize (NOH bel prize) — annual prize given by the Nobel Foundation for some great achievement in each of the following subjects: physics, chemistry, economics, medicine, literature, and for promoting world peace

population (pop yuh LAY shuhn) — the number of people living in one place or country

prejudice (PREJ uh diss) — an unfair or biased opinion

professional (pruh FESH uh nuhl) — a person who has special skills

refugee (ref yuh JEE) — a person who flees from one country to another to avoid war, disaster, or persecution

revolution (rev uh LOO shuhn) — sudden change that is often violent, and that leads to a change in the government or social system of a country

ritual (RICH oo uhl) — a set of actions performed as part of a religious or public ceremony

sari (SAH ree) — a long, often colorful, piece of cotton or silk that is draped around the body and worn as a dress

Sikh (SEEK) – someone who follows the religion of Sikhism

temperate (TEM pur it) — describes a climate that is not too hot or too cold

terrorist (TER uh ist) — person or organization that will use any means, however violent, to bring about their political goals

tropical (TROP uh kuhl) — describes a hot climate with heavy rainfall

turban (TUR buhn) — a scarf that is wound around the head

FURTHER INFORMATION

Places to Visit or Write

Little India
74th Street,
Jackson Heights, NY 11372
One of the largest Little Indias in the United States.

Vedanta Temple
2963 Webster Street,
San Francisco, CA 94117
Former Hindu temple with unusual architecture.

Books

South Asian Americans. Scott Ingram. World Almanac Library, 2007.

India. Joanne Mattern. Bridgestone Books, 2006.

Foods of India. Barbara Sheen. Kidhaven Press, 2007.

Gandhi: The Young Protester Who Founded a Nation. Ian Wilkinson. National Geographic Children's Books, 2005.

Websites to Visit

http://www.pbs.org/rootsinthesand/

Describes the hardships and successes of the first wave of Asian-Indian immigrants to the West Coast.

http://www.littleindia.com/

Online Indian-American magazine.

http://www.ancientindia.co.uk/index.html

Information about ancient India from the British Museum.

INDEX